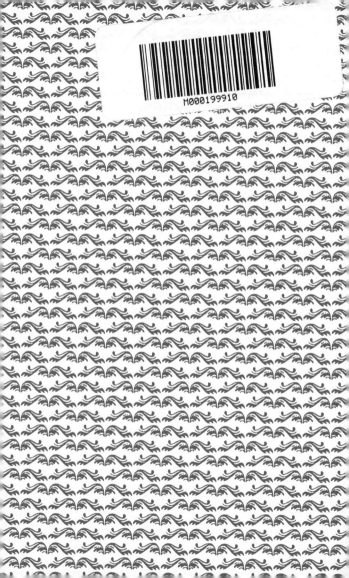

M000199910

Introduction

I determined to give a week's strict attention to each of the virtues successively.

1. TEMPERANCE. *Eat not to dullness; drink not to elevation.*

2. SILENCE. *Speak not but what may benefit others or yourself; avoid trifling conversation.*

3. ORDER. *Let all your things have their places; let each part of your business have its time.*

4. RESOLUTION. *Resolve to perform what you ought; perform without fail what you resolve.*

5. FRUGALITY. *Make no expense but to do good to others or yourself; i.e., waste nothing.*

6. INDUSTRY. *Lose no time; be always employ'd in something useful; cut off all unnecessary actions.*

7. SINCERITY. *Use no hurtful deceit; think innocently and justly, and, if you speak, speak accordingly.*

8. JUSTICE. *Wrong none by doing injuries, or omitting the benefits that are your duty.*

9. MODERATION. *Avoid extremes; forbear resenting injuries so much as you think they deserve.*

10. CLEANLINESS. *Tolerate no uncleanliness in body, clothes, or habitation.*

11. TRANQUILLITY. *Be not disturbed at trifles, or at accidents common or unavoidable.*

12. CHASTITY. *Rarely use venery but for health or offspring, never to dullness, weakness, or the injury of your own or another's peace or reputation.*

13. HUMILITY. *Imitate Jesus and Socrates.*

Thus, in the first week, my great guard was to avoid every the least offense against Temperance, leaving the other virtues to their ordinary chance, only marking every evening the faults of the day. Thus, if in the first week I could keep my first line, marked T, clear of spots, I suppos'd the habit of that virtue so much strengthen'd and its opposite weaken'd, that I might venture extending my attention to include the next, and for the following week keep both lines clear of spots. Proceeding thus to the last, I could go thro' a course complete in thirteen weeks, and four courses in a year. And like him who, having a garden to weed, does not attempt to eradicate all the bad herbs at once, which would exceed his reach and his strength, but works on one of the beds at a time, and, having accomplish'd the first, proceeds to a second, so I should have, I hoped, the encouraging pleasure of seeing on my pages the progress I made in virtue, by clearing successively my lines of their spots, till in the end, by a number of courses, I should be happy in viewing a clean book, after a thirteen weeks' daily examination.

TAKEN FROM Benjamin Franklin's *Book of Virtues*

Notes

Virtues

Eat not to dullness;
drink not to elevation.

	Sun.	M.	T.	W.	Th.	F.	S.
Tem.							
Sil.							
Ord.							
Res.							
Fru.							
Ind.							
Sinc.							
Jus.							
Mod.							
Clea.							
Tran.							
Chas.							
Hum.							

Notes

Virtues

Eat not to dullness;
drink not to elevation.

	Sun.	M.	T.	W.	Th.	F.	S.
Tem.							
Sil.							
Ord.							
Res.							
Fru.							
Ind.							
Sinc.							
Jus.							
Mod.							
Clea.							
Tran.							
Chas.							
Hum.							

Notes

Virtues

Eat not to dullness;
drink not to elevation.

	Sun.	M.	T.	W.	Th.	F.	S.
Tem.							
Sil.							
Ord.							
Res.							
Fru.							
Ind.							
Sinc.							
Jus.							
Mod.							
Clea.							
Tran.							
Chas.							
Hum.							

Notes

Virtues

Eat not to dullness;
drink not to elevation.

	Sun.	M.	T.	W.	Th.	F.	S.
Tem.							
Sil.							
Ord.							
Res.							
Fru.							
Ind.							
Sinc.							
Jus.							
Mod.							
Clea.							
Tran.							
Chas.							
Hum.							

Notes

Virtues

Eat not to dullness;
drink not to elevation.

	Sun.	M.	T.	W.	Th.	F.	S.
Tem.							
Sil.							
Ord.							
Res.							
Fru.							
Ind.							
Sinc.							
Jus.							
Mod.							
Clea.							
Tran.							
Chas.							
Hum.							

Notes

Virtues

Eat not to dullness;
drink not to elevation.

	Sun.	M.	T.	W.	Th.	F.	S.
Tem.							
Sil.							
Ord.							
Res.							
Fru.							
Ind.							
Sinc.							
Jus.							
Mod.							
Clea.							
Tran.							
Chas.							
Hum.							

Notes

Virtues

Eat not to dullness;
drink not to elevation.

	Sun.	M.	T.	W.	Th.	F.	S.
Tem.							
Sil.							
Ord.							
Res.							
Fru.							
Ind.							
Sinc.							
Jus.							
Mod.							
Clea.							
Tran.							
Chas.							
Hum.							

Notes

Virtues

Eat not to dullness;
drink not to elevation.

	Sun.	M.	T.	W.	Th.	F.	S.
Tem.							
Sil.							
Ord.							
Res.							
Fru.							
Ind.							
Sinc.							
Jus.							
Mod.							
Clea.							
Tran.							
Chas.							
Hum.							

Notes

Virtues

Eat not to dullness;
drink not to elevation.

	Sun.	M.	T.	W.	Th.	F.	S.
Tem.							
Sil.							
Ord.							
Res.							
Fru.							
Ind.							
Sinc.							
Jus.							
Mod.							
Clea.							
Tran.							
Chas.							
Hum.							

Notes

Virtues

Eat not to dullness;
drink not to elevation.

	Sun.	M.	T.	W.	Th.	F.	S.
Tem.							
Sil.							
Ord.							
Res.							
Fru.							
Ind.							
Sinc.							
Jus.							
Mod.							
Clea.							
Tran.							
Chas.							
Hum.							

Notes

Virtues

Eat not to dullness;
drink not to elevation.

	Sun.	M.	T.	W.	Th.	F.	S.
Tem.							
Sil.							
Ord.							
Res.							
Fru.							
Ind.							
Sinc.							
Jus.							
Mod.							
Clea.							
Tran.							
Chas.							
Hum.							

Notes

Virtues

Eat not to dullness;
drink not to elevation.

	Sun.	M.	T.	W.	Th.	F.	S.
Tem.							
Sil.							
Ord.							
Res.							
Fru.							
Ind.							
Sinc.							
Jus.							
Mod.							
Clea.							
Tran.							
Chas.							
Hum.							

Notes

Virtues

Eat not to dullness;
drink not to elevation.

	Sun.	M.	T.	W.	Th.	F.	S.
Tem.							
Sil.							
Ord.							
Res.							
Fru.							
Ind.							
Sinc.							
Jus.							
Mod.							
Clea.							
Tran.							
Chas.							
Hum.							

Notes

Virtues

Eat not to dullness;
drink not to elevation.

	Sun.	M.	T.	W.	Th.	F.	S.
Tem.							
Sil.							
Ord.							
Res.							
Fru.							
Ind.							
Sinc.							
Jus.							
Mod.							
Clea.							
Tran.							
Chas.							
Hum.							

Notes

Virtues

Eat not to dullness;
drink not to elevation.

	Sun.	M.	T.	W.	Th.	F.	S.
Tem.							
Sil.							
Ord.							
Res.							
Fru.							
Ind.							
Sinc.							
Jus.							
Mod.							
Clea.							
Tran.							
Chas.							
Hum.							

Notes

Virtues

Eat not to dullness;
drink not to elevation.

	Sun.	M.	T.	W.	Th.	F.	S.
Tem.							
Sil.							
Ord.							
Res.							
Fru.							
Ind.							
Sinc.							
Jus.							
Mod.							
Clea.							
Tran.							
Chas.							
Hum.							

Notes

Virtues

Eat not to dullness;
drink not to elevation.

	Sun.	M.	T.	W.	Th.	F.	S.
Tem.							
Sil.							
Ord.							
Res.							
Fru.							
Ind.							
Sinc.							
Jus.							
Mod.							
Clea.							
Tran.							
Chas.							
Hum.							

Notes

Virtues

Eat not to dullness;
drink not to elevation.

	Sun.	M.	T.	W.	Th.	F.	S.
Tem.							
Sil.							
Ord.							
Res.							
Fru.							
Ind.							
Sinc.							
Jus.							
Mod.							
Clea.							
Tran.							
Chas.							
Hum.							

Notes

Virtues

Eat not to dullness;
drink not to elevation.

	Sun.	M.	T.	W.	Th.	F.	S.
Tem.							
Sil.							
Ord.							
Res.							
Fru.							
Ind.							
Sinc.							
Jus.							
Mod.							
Clea.							
Tran.							
Chas.							
Hum.							

Notes

Virtues

Eat not to dullness;
drink not to elevation.

	Sun.	M.	T.	W.	Th.	F.	S.
Tem.							
Sil.							
Ord.							
Res.							
Fru.							
Ind.							
Sinc.							
Jus.							
Mod.							
Clea.							
Tran.							
Chas.							
Hum.							

Notes

Virtues

Eat not to dullness;
drink not to elevation.

	Sun.	M.	T.	W.	Th.	F.	S.
Tem.							
Sil.							
Ord.							
Res.							
Fru.							
Ind.							
Sinc.							
Jus.							
Mod.							
Clea.							
Tran.							
Chas.							
Hum.							

Notes

Virtues

Eat not to dullness;
drink not to elevation.

	Sun.	M.	T.	W.	Th.	F.	S.
Tem.							
Sil.							
Ord.							
Res.							
Fru.							
Ind.							
Sinc.							
Jus.							
Mod.							
Clea.							
Tran.							
Chas.							
Hum.							

Notes

Virtues

Eat not to dullness;
drink not to elevation.

	Sun.	M.	T.	W.	Th.	F.	S.
Tem.							
Sil.							
Ord.							
Res.							
Fru.							
Ind.							
Sinc.							
Jus.							
Mod.							
Clea.							
Tran.							
Chas.							
Hum.							

Notes

Virtues

Eat not to dullness;
drink not to elevation.

	Sun.	M.	T.	W.	Th.	F.	S.
Tem.							
Sil.							
Ord.							
Res.							
Fru.							
Ind.							
Sinc.							
Jus.							
Mod.							
Clea.							
Tran.							
Chas.							
Hum.							

Notes

Virtues

Eat not to dullness;
drink not to elevation.

	Sun.	M.	T.	W.	Th.	F.	S.
Tem.							
Sil.							
Ord.							
Res.							
Fru.							
Ind.							
Sinc.							
Jus.							
Mod.							
Clea.							
Tran.							
Chas.							
Hum.							

Notes

Virtues

Eat not to dullness;
drink not to elevation.

	Sun.	M.	T.	W.	Th.	F.	S.
Tem.							
Sil.							
Ord.							
Res.							
Fru.							
Ind.							
Sinc.							
Jus.							
Mod.							
Clea.							
Tran.							
Chas.							
Hum.							

Notes

Virtues

Eat not to dullness;
drink not to elevation.

	Sun.	M.	T.	W.	Th.	F.	S.
Tem.							
Sil.							
Ord.							
Res.							
Fru.							
Ind.							
Sinc.							
Jus.							
Mod.							
Clea.							
Tran.							
Chas.							
Hum.							

Notes

Virtues

Eat not to dullness;
drink not to elevation.

	Sun.	M.	T.	W.	Th.	F.	S.
Tem.							
Sil.							
Ord.							
Res.							
Fru.							
Ind.							
Sinc.							
Jus.							
Mod.							
Clea.							
Tran.							
Chas.							
Hum.							

Notes

Virtues

Eat not to dullness;
drink not to elevation.

	Sun.	M.	T.	W.	Th.	F.	S.
Tem.							
Sil.							
Ord.							
Res.							
Fru.							
Ind.							
Sinc.							
Jus.							
Mod.							
Clea.							
Tran.							
Chas.							
Hum.							

Notes

Virtues

Eat not to dullness;
drink not to elevation.

	Sun.	M.	T.	W.	Th.	F.	S.
Tem.							
Sil.							
Ord.							
Res.							
Fru.							
Ind.							
Sinc.							
Jus.							
Mod.							
Clea.							
Tran.							
Chas.							
Hum.							

Notes

Virtues

Eat not to dullness;
drink not to elevation.

	Sun.	M.	T.	W.	Th.	F.	S.
Tem.							
Sil.							
Ord.							
Res.							
Fru.							
Ind.							
Sinc.							
Jus.							
Mod.							
Clea.							
Tran.							
Chas.							
Hum.							

Notes

Virtues

Eat not to dullness;
drink not to elevation.

	Sun.	M.	T.	W.	Th.	F.	S.
Tem.							
Sil.							
Ord.							
Res.							
Fru.							
Ind.							
Sinc.							
Jus.							
Mod.							
Clea.							
Tran.							
Chas.							
Hum.							

Notes

Virtues

Eat not to dullness;
drink not to elevation.

	Sun.	M.	T.	W.	Th.	F.	S.
Tem.							
Sil.							
Ord.							
Res.							
Fru.							
Ind.							
Sinc.							
Jus.							
Mod.							
Clea.							
Tran.							
Chas.							
Hum.							

Notes

Virtues

Eat not to dullness;
drink not to elevation.

	Sun.	M.	T.	W.	Th.	F.	S.
Tem.							
Sil.							
Ord.							
Res.							
Fru.							
Ind.							
Sinc.							
Jus.							
Mod.							
Clea.							
Tran.							
Chas.							
Hum.							

Notes

Virtues

Eat not to dullness;
drink not to elevation.

	Sun.	M.	T.	W.	Th.	F.	S.
Tem.							
Sil.							
Ord.							
Res.							
Fru.							
Ind.							
Sinc.							
Jus.							
Mod.							
Clea.							
Tran.							
Chas.							
Hum.							

Notes

Virtues

Eat not to dullness;
drink not to elevation.

	Sun.	M.	T.	W.	Th.	F.	S.
Tem.							
Sil.							
Ord.							
Res.							
Fru.							
Ind.							
Sinc.							
Jus.							
Mod.							
Clea.							
Tran.							
Chas.							
Hum.							

Notes

Virtues

Eat not to dullness;
drink not to elevation.

	Sun.	M.	T.	W.	Th.	F.	S.
Tem.							
Sil.							
Ord.							
Res.							
Fru.							
Ind.							
Sinc.							
Jus.							
Mod.							
Clea.							
Tran.							
Chas.							
Hum.							

Notes

Virtues

Eat not to dullness;
drink not to elevation.

	Sun.	M.	T.	W.	Th.	F.	S.
Tem.							
Sil.							
Ord.							
Res.							
Fru.							
Ind.							
Sinc.							
Jus.							
Mod.							
Clea.							
Tran.							
Chas.							
Hum.							

Notes

Virtues

Eat not to dullness;
drink not to elevation.

	Sun.	M.	T.	W.	Th.	F.	S.
Tem.							
Sil.							
Ord.							
Res.							
Fru.							
Ind.							
Sinc.							
Jus.							
Mod.							
Clea.							
Tran.							
Chas.							
Hum.							

Notes

Virtues

Eat not to dullness;
drink not to elevation.

	Sun.	M.	T.	W.	Th.	F.	S.
Tem.							
Sil.							
Ord.							
Res.							
Fru.							
Ind.							
Sinc.							
Jus.							
Mod.							
Clea.							
Tran.							
Chas.							
Hum.							

Notes

Virtues

Eat not to dullness;
drink not to elevation.

	Sun.	M.	T.	W.	Th.	F.	S.
Tem.							
Sil.							
Ord.							
Res.							
Fru.							
Ind.							
Sinc.							
Jus.							
Mod.							
Clea.							
Tran.							
Chas.							
Hum.							

Notes

Virtues

Eat not to dullness;
drink not to elevation.

	Sun.	M.	T.	W.	Th.	F.	S.
Tem.							
Sil.							
Ord.							
Res.							
Fru.							
Ind.							
Sinc.							
Jus.							
Mod.							
Clea.							
Tran.							
Chas.							
Hum.							

Notes

Virtues

Eat not to dullness;
drink not to elevation.

	Sun.	M.	T.	W.	Th.	F.	S.
Tem.							
Sil.							
Ord.							
Res.							
Fru.							
Ind.							
Sinc.							
Jus.							
Mod.							
Clea.							
Tran.							
Chas.							
Hum.							

Notes

Virtues

Eat not to dullness;
drink not to elevation.

	Sun.	M.	T.	W.	Th.	F.	S.
Tem.							
Sil.							
Ord.							
Res.							
Fru.							
Ind.							
Sinc.							
Jus.							
Mod.							
Clea.							
Tran.							
Chas.							
Hum.							

Notes

Virtues

Eat not to dullness;
drink not to elevation.

	Sun.	M.	T.	W.	Th.	F.	S.
Tem.							
Sil.							
Ord.							
Res.							
Fru.							
Ind.							
Sinc.							
Jus.							
Mod.							
Clea.							
Tran.							
Chas.							
Hum.							

Notes

Virtues

Eat not to dullness;
drink not to elevation.

	Sun.	M.	T.	W.	Th.	F.	S.
Tem.							
Sil.							
Ord.							
Res.							
Fru.							
Ind.							
Sinc.							
Jus.							
Mod.							
Clea.							
Tran.							
Chas.							
Hum.							

Notes

Virtues

Eat not to dullness;
drink not to elevation.

	Sun.	M.	T.	W.	Th.	F.	S.
Tem.							
Sil.							
Ord.							
Res.							
Fru.							
Ind.							
Sinc.							
Jus.							
Mod.							
Clea.							
Tran.							
Chas.							
Hum.							

Notes

Virtues

Eat not to dullness;
drink not to elevation.

	Sun.	M.	T.	W.	Th.	F.	S.
Tem.							
Sil.							
Ord.							
Res.							
Fru.							
Ind.							
Sinc.							
Jus.							
Mod.							
Clea.							
Tran.							
Chas.							
Hum.							

Notes

Virtues

Eat not to dullness;
drink not to elevation.

	Sun.	M.	T.	W.	Th.	F.	S.
Tem.							
Sil.							
Ord.							
Res.							
Fru.							
Ind.							
Sinc.							
Jus.							
Mod.							
Clea.							
Tran.							
Chas.							
Hum.							

Notes

Virtues

Eat not to dullness;
drink not to elevation.

	Sun.	M.	T.	W.	Th.	F.	S.
Tem.							
Sil.							
Ord.							
Res.							
Fru.							
Ind.							
Sinc.							
Jus.							
Mod.							
Clea.							
Tran.							
Chas.							
Hum.							

Notes

Virtues

Eat not to dullness;
drink not to elevation.

	Sun.	M.	T.	W.	Th.	F.	S.
Tem.							
Sil.							
Ord.							
Res.							
Fru.							
Ind.							
Sinc.							
Jus.							
Mod.							
Clea.							
Tran.							
Chas.							
Hum.							

Virtues

Eat not to dullness;
drink not to elevation.

	Sun.	M.	T.	W.	Th.	F.	S.
Tem.							
Sil.							
Ord.							
Res.							
Fru.							
Ind.							
Sinc.							
Jus.							
Mod.							
Clea.							
Tran.							
Chas.							
Hum.							

Notes

978-1-4290-9392-7

Copyright © 2016 Applewood Books, Inc.

"Portrait of Benjamin Franklin," engraving
by Henry Bryan Hall Sr., from the original portrait
painted from life by J. A. Duplessis in 1783.

MANUFACTURED IN THE UNITED STATES OF AMERICA

BENJAMIN FRANKLIN'S

VIRTUES

JOURNAL

A Companion to

Benjamin Franklin's

Book of Virtues

Applewood Books
Carlisle, Massachusetts